THE
MOVIE
BOOK
OF
ANSWERS™

CAROL BOLT

NEW YORK   BOSTON

To Christina Anne Lee. Thank you for your love and understanding.
Let's stay up late and watch movies forever.

———————————

Copyright © 2001, 2018 by Carol Bolt

Cover design by Kapo Ng.

Cover copyright © 2018 by Hachette Book Group, Inc.

Hachette Books
Hachette Book Group
1290 Avenue of the Americas, New York, NY 10104
hachettebooks.com
twitter.com/hachettebooks

Originally published in hardcover by Hyperion in October 2001

Updated edition: October 2018

Hachette Books is a division of Hachette Book Group, Inc.
The Hachette Books name and logo are trademarks of Hachette Book Group, Inc.

The publisher is not responsible for websites (or their content) that are not owned by the publisher.

The Hachette Speakers Bureau provides a wide range of authors for speaking events.
To find out more, go to www.hachettespeakersbureau.com or call (866) 376-6591.

Print book interior design by KimShala Wilson.

Library of Congress Control Number: 2018952961

ISBNs: 978-0-31644-992-2 (updated edition); 978-0-316-44994-6 (electronic book)

Printed in the United States of America

LSC-C

10 9 8 7 6 5 4 3 2 1

HOW TO USE *The Movie Book of Answers*™

1. Hold the **closed** book in your hand, on your lap, or on a table.

2. Take 10 or 15 seconds to **concentrate** on your question. Questions should be phrased **closed-end**, e.g., "Is the job I'm applying for the right one?" or "Should I travel this weekend?"

3. While visualizing or speaking your question (one question at a time), place **one hand** palm down on the book's front cover and **stroke the edge** of the pages, back to front.

4. When you **sense** the time is right, **open** the book and there will be your answer.

5. **Repeat** the process for as many questions as you have.

Got questions? This book has the answers.

Carol Bolt is a professional artist living in Seattle.

BRAG ABOUT IT

—Sam Spade, *The Maltese Falcon*

BAA-RAM-EWE,
TO YOUR OWN BREED,
YOUR FLEECE,
YOUR CLAN BE TRUE

—Sheep, *Babe*

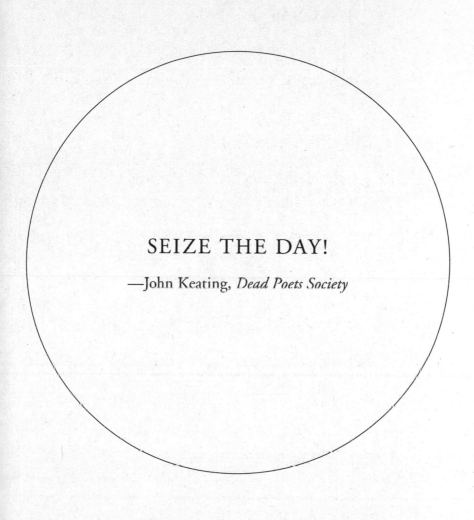

SEIZE THE DAY!

—John Keating, *Dead Poets Society*

FASTEN YOUR SEAT BELT,

IT [COULD] BE

A BUMPY NIGHT

—Margo Channing, *All About Eve*

HAVE A PLAN

—Willi, *Lifeboat*

YOU GOTTA DRAW
FASTER THAN SOMEBODY ELSE

—Cole Thorton, *El Dorado*

AH, SWEET MYSTERY OF LIFE
AT LAST [YOU] FOUND [IT]!

—Elizabeth, *Young Frankenstein*

[BE] READY FOR [YOUR] CLOSE-UP

—Norma Desmond, *Sunset Boulevard*

DON'T DO ANYTHING HASTY

—Angela Vickers, *A Place in the Sun*

WHAT YOU SAY [WILL] COUNT

—Sean Thornton, *The Quiet Man*

PUT [THE] SHOE ON THE OTHER
FOOT

—King Marchand, *Victor/Victoria*

GET A SHOT AT IT

—Jimmy "Popeye" Doyle, *The French Connection*

YOU WILL HAVE [IT]
WHEN YOU NEED IT

—Nickie Ferrante, *An Affair to Remember*

TOO MUCH DEVOTION [COULD]
GET YOU IRRITABLE

—Brick, *Cat on a Hot Tin Roof*

BE CONTENT WITH
WHAT YOU HAVE

—Alice Tripp, *A Place in the Sun*

FOLLOW THE LEAD

—Trevor Beckwith, *Best in Show*

YOU'LL NEED A FRIEND

—Fiedler, *The Spy Who Came in From the Cold*

IT [COULD BE] A RED HERRING

—Miss Scarlet, *Clue*

[DON'T] LET YOURSELF
ATTACH MUCH IMPORTANCE
TO THESE THINGS

—Kasper Gutman, *The Maltese Falcon*

THIS BUSINESS REQUIRES A CERTAIN AMOUNT OF FINESSE

—Jake "J. J." Gittes, *Chinatown*

COPY THE MASTERS,
LEARN THEIR SECRETS

—Charles Bonnet, *How to Steal a Million*

WHAT ELSE COULD YA DO?

—Belle Rosen, *The Poseidon Adventure*

[DON'T] IGNORE IT

—Melanie Daniels, *The Birds*

SOMETIMES [THINGS] NEED

A LOT OF WATCHING

—Sergeant Jack Graham, *Shadow of a Doubt*

[YOU] CAN MAKE IT

—Dr. Ellie Sattler, *Jurassic Park*

REASSEMBLE YOUR FACULTIES
AND START PACKING

—Phileas Fogg, *Around the World in 80 Days*

SIT HERE [AWHILE]

—Mrs. Bates, *Psycho*

ALWAYS KNOW WHEN TO LEAVE

—Sipsey, *Fried Green Tomatoes*

SOME PEOPLE [MIGHT]
PAY A LOT OF MONEY
FOR THAT INFORMATION

—Michael Corleone, *The Godfather*

NOBODY'S GONNA RAIN ON [YOUR] PARADE

—Fanny Brice, *Funny Girl*

[DON'T] LET [A] GOLDEN
MOMENT PASS YOU BY

—Billy, *Carousel*

GO WITH THE FLOW

—Dr. Michaels, *Fantastic Voyage*

IT'S PERFECT

—Joanna Eberhart, *The Stepford Wives*

REVEL IN YOUR TIME

—Dr. Eldon Tyrell, *Blade Runner*

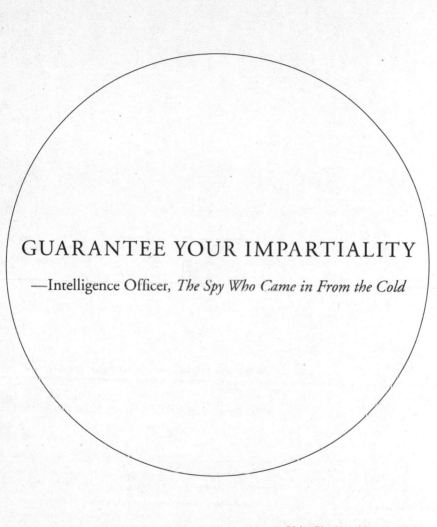

GUARANTEE YOUR IMPARTIALITY

—Intelligence Officer, *The Spy Who Came in From the Cold*

[BE] HIP ABOUT TIME

—Captain America, *Easy Rider*

MAKE TIME

—Frank Stark, *Rebel Without a Cause*

THE LONGER YOU WAIT,

THE MORE SENSE YOU GET

—Jerry, *The Divorcee*

WHAD' [ELSE] YA
GOT THERE IN YER POKE?

—Rooster Cogburn, *True Grit*

DON'T DILLYDALLY

—Phileas Fogg, *Around the World in 80 Days*

TAKE IT EASY,
BUT TAKE IT

—Radio Announcer, *Midnight Cowboy*

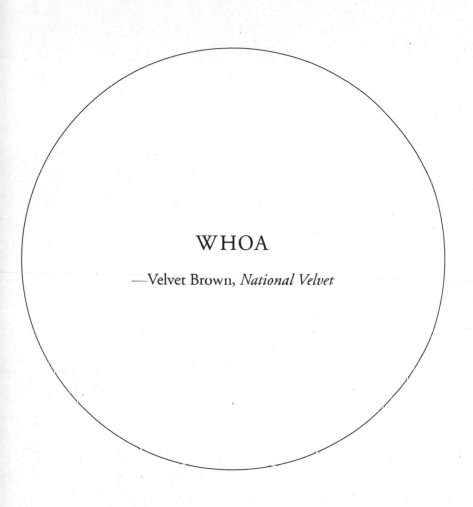

WHOA

—Velvet Brown, *National Velvet*

'THERE'LL BE NO ONE TO STOP

[YOU]

—Darth Vader, *Star Wars*

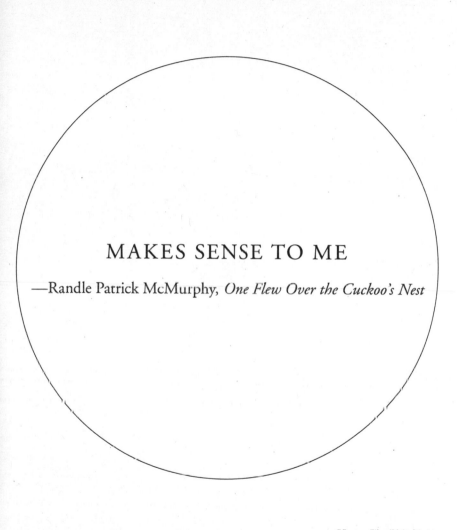

MAKES SENSE TO ME

—Randle Patrick McMurphy, *One Flew Over the Cuckoo's Nest*

FIND A WAY TO MAKE IT WORK

—George Fields, *Tootsie*

NO[BODY] SHOULD KNOW TOO
MUCH
ABOUT HIS OWN DESTINY

—Doc Brown, *Back to the Future*

LEAD [THIS]

—Pike Bishop, *The Wild Bunch*

A TANTALIZING PLUM HAS
DROPPED INTO [YOUR] LAP

—Carol Lipton, *Manhattan Murder Mystery*

THE CALENDAR TAKES CARE OF EVERYTHING

EVERYTHING

—Maerose, *Prizzi's Honor*

[MIGHT TAKE] LONGER THAN
YOU FIGURED

—Sergeant Sefton, *Stalag 17*

WHAT YOU'RE LOOKING FOR [IS] IN YOUR OWN BACKYARD

—Dorothy, *The Wizard of Oz*

YOU PAYS YER MONEY,
YOU TAKES YER CHOICE

—Charlie, *The African Queen*

NO

—Mrs. Bates, *Psycho*

DON'T GO [IT] ALONE

—Steve, *Singles*

TAKE YOUR TIME IN PICKING

—Buck Laughlin, *Best in Show*

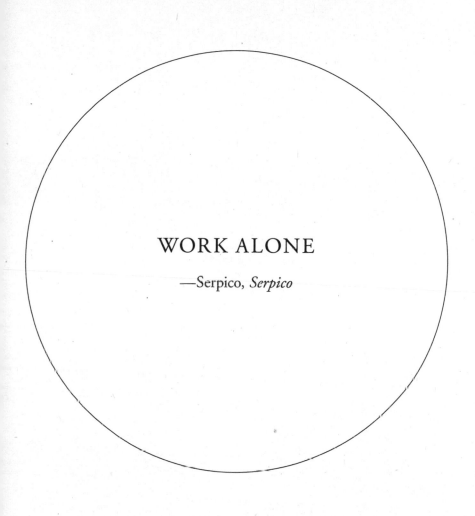

WORK ALONE

—Serpico, *Serpico*

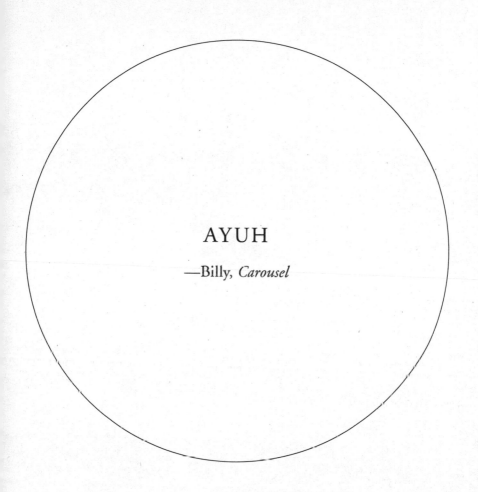

AYUH

—Billy, *Carousel*

TURN [IT] INTO VICTORY

—Colonel Nicholson, *The Bridge on the River Kwai*

ONCE YOU HAVE FOUND [IT],
NEVER LET [IT] GO

—Emile, *South Pacific*

RECOGNIZE YOUR TALENTS

—Elastigirl, *The Incredibles*

I COULDN'T IMAGINE A BETTER
FATE

—Phil Connors, *Groundhog Day*

IT'S NOT [A] HARD SHOT

—Vincent, *The Color of Money*

YOU COULD BE A CONTENDER

—Terry Malloy, *On the Waterfront*

[HAVE] AS MANY NOTES AS
REQUIRED;
NO MORE, NO LESS

—Mozart, *Amadeus*

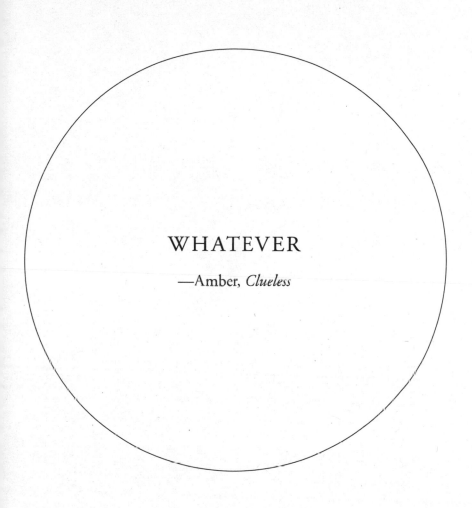

WHATEVER

—Amber, *Clueless*

YOU'RE GONNA NEED
A BIGGER BOAT

—Brody, *Jaws*

SEE WHERE IT LEADS

—Colonel Mustard, *Clue*

IN [THE] MOST DELIGHTFUL WAY

—Mary Poppins, *Mary Poppins*

LOOK FOR THE
BARE NECESSITIES

—Baloo the Bear, *The Jungle Book*

THE FUTURE IS NOT SET

—Kyle Reese, *The Terminator*

[YOU] GOT NO STRINGS
TO HOLD [YOU] DOWN

—Pinocchio, *Pinocchio*

TAKE ALL THE PIECES,
PUT THEM TOGETHER

—Inspector Peterson, *Mildred Pierce*

[THAT'S] QUITE A PARCEL

—Dr. Horace Lynnton, *Giant*

[DON'T] SAY IT LIKE IT'S A NEGATIVE THING

—Alvy Singer, *Annie Hall*

IT COULD WORK

—Dr. Frederick Frankenstein, *Young Frankenstein*

REMEMBER THE LITTLE THINGS

—Charlie Babbitt, *Rain Man*

ACKNOWLEDGE YOUR RESPONSIBILITIES

—Alex, *Fatal Attraction*

STAY ON TARGET

—Fighter Pilot Gold #5, *Star Wars*

THIS [WILL BE] SOMETHING
OF AN EXPEDITION

—Colonel Harry Brighton, *Lawrence of Arabia*

YOU TELL ME WHAT YOU KNOW AND I'LL CONFIRM

—Deep Throat, *All the President's Men*

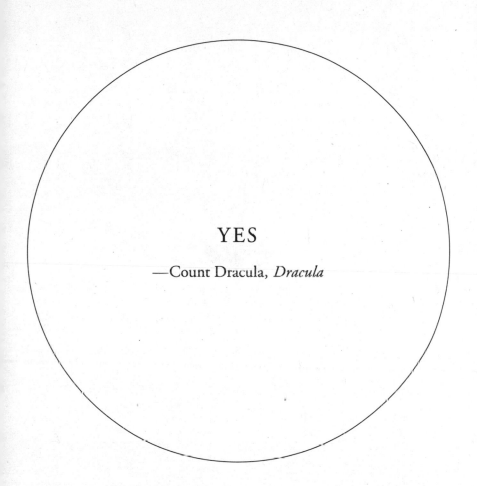

YES

—Count Dracula, *Dracula*

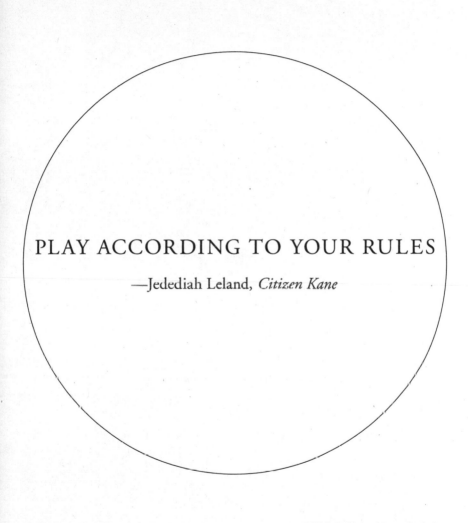

PLAY ACCORDING TO YOUR RULES

—Jedediah Leland, *Citizen Kane*

GET IT IN THE LARGE, ECONOMY SIZE

—Joe, *Tarantula*

IT MAKES PERFECT SENSE

—Agent J, *Men in Black*

[MAKE] IT THE BIGGEST THING
IN THE WORLD

—Carl Denham, *King Kong*

MORE, MORE, MORE!

—Janet, *The Rocky Horror Picture Show*

SPEND A LOT OF TIME SETTIN' THIS ONE UP

—Sal, *The French Connection*

COMMUNICATE MORE FULLY

—Edward R. Murrow, *Good Night, and Good Luck*

THE WHOLE POINT
[COULD BE] LOST
IF YOU KEEP IT A SECRET

—Dr. Strangelove, *Dr. Strangelove or: How I Learned to Stop Worrying and Love the Bomb*

KEEP GOING

—Thelma Dickinson, *Thelma & Louise*

RELAX, DAMMIT, RELAX

—Oscar, *The Odd Couple*

YOU MUST HAVE HOPE

—Lilia, *The Ten Commandments*

IT'LL PROBABLY TURN OUT TO BE A VERY SIMPLE THING

—Mr. Rawlston, *Citizen Kane*

[YOU] HAVE SUCH A GOOD CHANCE

—Atticus Finch, *To Kill a Mockingbird*

BEEEEEEE . . . GOOOOOOD

—E.T.. *E.T. the Extra-Terrestrial*

FRANKLY MY DEAR,
[YOU] DON'T GIVE A DAMN

—Rhett Butler, *Gone with the Wind*

MAYBE NOT TODAY,
MAYBE NOT TOMORROW,
BUT SOON

—Rick, *Casablanca*

LET IT GO

—Gandalf, *Lord of the Rings: The Fellowship of the Ring*

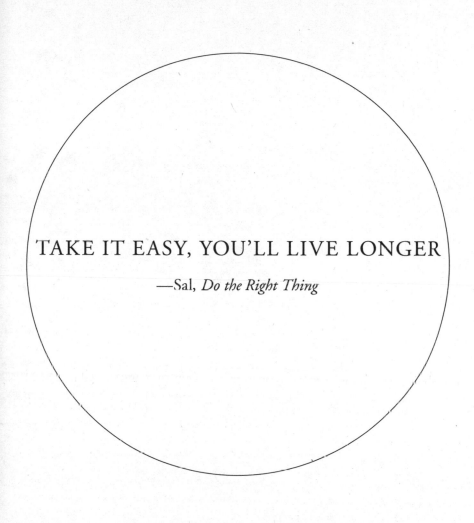

TAKE IT EASY, YOU'LL LIVE LONGER

—Sal, *Do the Right Thing*

SEE THE RACE TO ITS END

—Eric Liddell, *Chariots of Fire*

THE FORCE WILL BE WITH YOU, ALWAYS

—Ben (Obi-Wan) Kenobi, *Star Wars*

EXPECT THE BEST

—Debbie, *Singles*

CUT A FEW [NOTES] AND IT WILL
BE PERFECT

—Emperor Joseph II, *Amadeus*

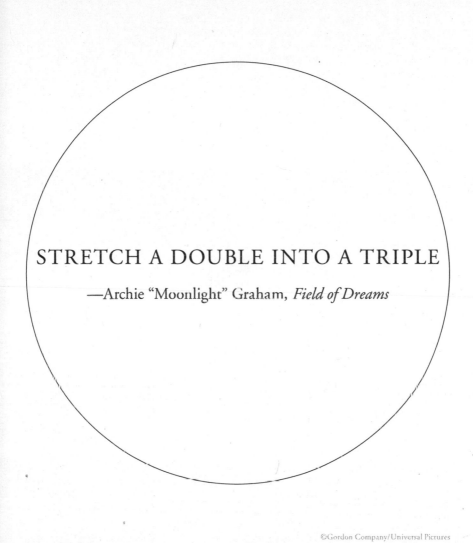

STRETCH A DOUBLE INTO A TRIPLE

—Archie "Moonlight" Graham, *Field of Dreams*

[IT] COULD TAKE YOU ANYWHERE

—Forrest Gump, *Forrest Gump*

PLAY NICE

—Woody, *Toy Story*

WHEN ARE [YOU] GONNA HAVE
SOME FUN?

—Oscar, *The Odd Couple*

SOMETHING [MAY]
ATTACH ITSELF TO [YOU]

—Dallas, *Alien*

DISCOVER A NEW SYSTEM OF COMMUNICATION

—Gertrudis, *Like Water for Chocolate*

SHARE [YOUR] PARTY LINE

—Jan Morrow, *Pillow Talk*

THE THING AIN'T THE RING, IT'S THE PLAY

—Jake La Motta, *Raging Bull*

STICK TO ESTABLISHED
PROCEDURES

—Dr. Jeremy Stone, *The Andromeda Strain*

[IT'LL] SOUND BETTER IN FRENCH

—Jerry Mulligan, *An American in Paris*

ALL MY READINGS POINT TO
SOMETHING BIG ON THE HORIZON

—Dr. Egon Spengler, *Ghostbusters*

MAKE AN OFFER [THEY] CAN'T
REFUSE

—Michael Corleone, *The Godfather*

YOU'RE GONNA KNOW WHERE IT'S AT

—Luz Benedict, *Giant*

CUT THIS SHORT

—Otis B. Driftwood, *A Night at the Opera*

SEE WHAT THE MAJORITY THINKS

—Max Bialystock, *The Producers*

THERE WON'T BE ANY TROUBLE

— Chris Adams, *The Magnificent Seven*

IT REQUIRES SOME SPECIAL
QUALITY OF EFFORT

—Monsignor Ryan, *Guess Who's Coming to Dinner*

YOU'VE GOT ALL THE FACTS

—Juror 3, *12 Angry Men*

[YOU] GOT SO MUCH,
GIVE SOME AWAY

—Charity Hope Valentine, *Sweet Charity*

[START WITH] THIRTY MINUTES OF SOMETHING WONDERFUL

—Shelby, *Steel Magnolias*

DON'T GET IN THE WAY

—Jesus Christ, *The Last Temptation of Christ*

LOVE THE DOING

—Roark, *The Fountainhead*

KEEP IT TO YOURSELF

—Stan, *The Conversation*

[WHAT] YOU DO
COULD HAVE REPERCUSSIONS
ON FUTURE EVENTS

—Doc Brown, *Back to the Future*

YEAH, . . . BITCHIN'

—Jeff Spicoli, *Fast Times at Ridgemont High*

YOU LOOK STRONG ENOUGH

—Moscs, *The Ten Commandments*

MY GOODNESS, [WOULDN'T] IT HELP?

—Lorelei Lee, *Gentlemen Prefer Blondes*

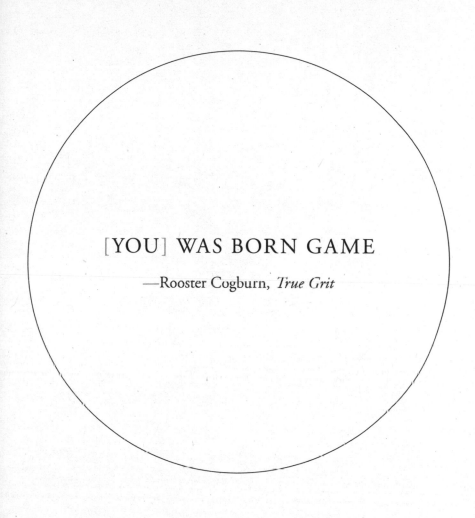

[YOU] WAS BORN GAME

—Rooster Cogburn, *True Grit*

STOP OFF FOR A QUICK ONE EN ROUTE

—James Bond, *Goldfinger*

STAY COOL

—John Milner, *American Graffiti*

[BE] FAST ON THE DRAW

—Wyatt Earp, *Gunfight at the O.K. Corral*

IT'LL [BE] ABOUT THE BIG PICTURE

—Ed Wood, *Ed Wood*

PLAY AS WELL AS YOU CAN

—Maude, *Harold and Maude*

HAVE A WONDERFUL TIME, WHOEVER [YOU'RE] WITH

—Elwood P. Dowd, *Harvey*

[THAT'S] A TARGET-RICH ENVIRONMENT

ENVIRONMENT

—Maverick, *Top Gun*

FIND A REAL-LIFE [THING]
THAT MAKES [YOU] FEEL
LIKE TIFFANY'S

—Holly Golightly, *Breakfast at Tiffany's*

[DON'T] BE HARD TO REACH

—D.A. Harvey Dent, *The Dark Knight*

IT'S A BEGINNING

—Viola De Lesseps, *Shakespeare in Love*

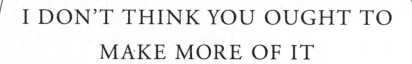

I DON'T THINK YOU OUGHT TO MAKE MORE OF IT

—Dr. Danny Kauffman, *Invasion of the Body Snatchers*

[YOU'RE] GOING TO HAVE TO BREAK A FEW RULES

—Woody, *Toy Story*

IF YOU WANT IT,
THROW A LASSO AROUND IT
AND PULL IT DOWN

—George Bailey, *It's a Wonderful Life*

[YOU] HAVE NOTHING TO LOSE

Lester Burnham, *American Beauty*

KEEP YOUR MIND OPEN TO ANYTHING

—Colonel Tom Edwards, *Plan 9 from Outer Space*

GET OUT OF TOWN
AND LET YOUR HAIR DOWN

—Thelma Dickinson, *Thelma & Louise*

BROWSE AROUND [A LITTLE MORE]

—Mark Zuckerberg, *The Social Network*

SOMETIMES YOU GOTTA LOSE
YOURSELF
'FORE YOU CAN FIND ANYTHING

—Lewis Medlock, *Deliverance*

DO YA FEEL LUCKY?

WELL, DO YA?

—Harry Callahan, *Dirty Harry*

HAVE SOMETHING TO FALL
BACK ON

—Bob, *My Own Private Idaho*

STRUT YOUR STUFF

—Corny Collins, *Hairspray*

[YOU MAY] NOT BE ABLE TO DO
IT [IF IT'S] DARK

—Heather Donahue, *The Blair Witch Project*

THE COAST IS CLEAR

—Marlin, *Finding Nemo*

IT [COULD] BE BOGUS

—Duckie, *Pretty in Pink*

OH, YES, YOU CAN . . .
YOU MUST

—Captain Von Trapp, *The Sound of Music*

GO WHILE THE GOIN'S GOOD

—Charlie, *The African Queen*

SHOW ['EM] WHAT YOU'RE MADE OF

—Roy Batty, *Blade Runner*

IT'S GONNA BE LIKE MONEY
FROM HOME

—Joe Buck, *Midnight Cowboy*

SEE WHO'S AROUND

—Father Dyer, *The Exorcist*

IT'LL [BE] IMPORTANT TO [YOU]

—Riggan Thomson, *Birdman or (The Unexpected Virtue of*

Ignorance)

WAIT FOR THE RIGHT MOMENT

Lionel Logue, *The King's Speech*

CHOOSE A LOVELY SPOT FOR [A] MEETING

—Karen Holmes, *From Here to Eternity*

DEPEND ON THE KINDNESS OF STRANGERS

STRANGERS

—Blanche DuBois, *A Streetcar Named Desire*

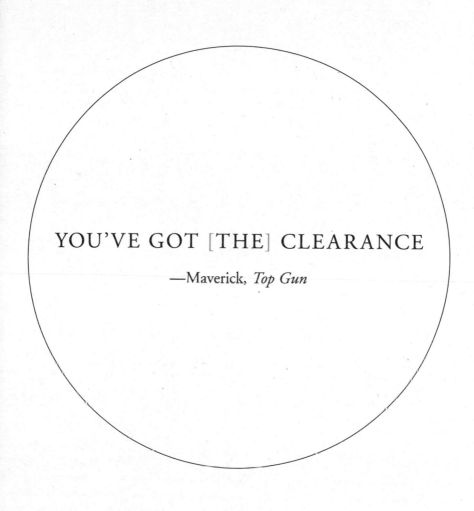

YOU'VE GOT [THE] CLEARANCE

—Maverick, *Top Gun*

A LITTLE DAB'LL DO YA!

—Randle Patrick McMurphy, *One Flew Over the Cuckoo's Nest*

YOU'RE DARNED TOOTIN'!

—Jerry Lundegaard, *Fargo*

PRETEND IT'S [YOUR] MAGIC
POWER

—Suzy, *Moonrise Kingdom*

SHOW RESPECT

—Dr. Alan Grant, *Jurassic Park*

[YOU'RE] GONNA WANNA LOAD THE BASES

—Shoeless Joe Jackson, *Field of Dreams*

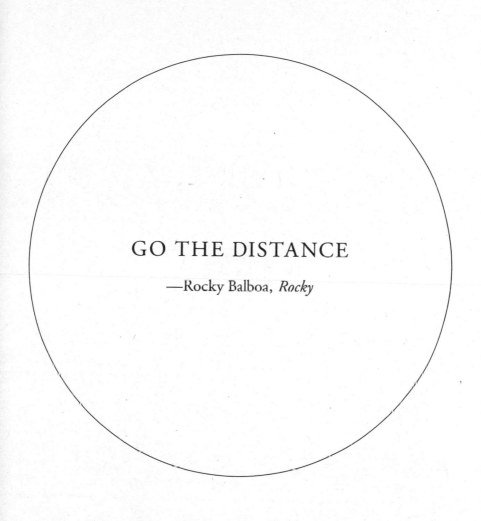

GO THE DISTANCE

—Rocky Balboa, *Rocky*

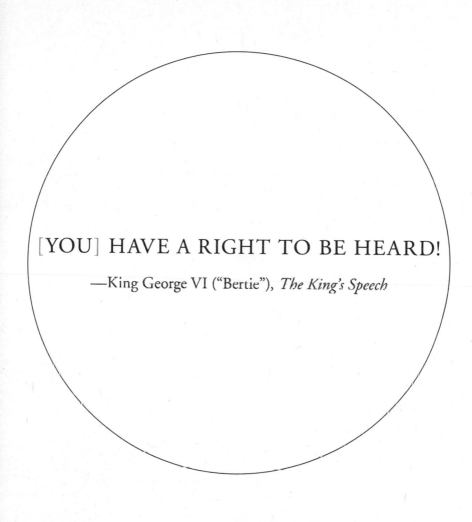

[YOU] HAVE A RIGHT TO BE HEARD!

—King George VI ("Bertie"), *The King's Speech*

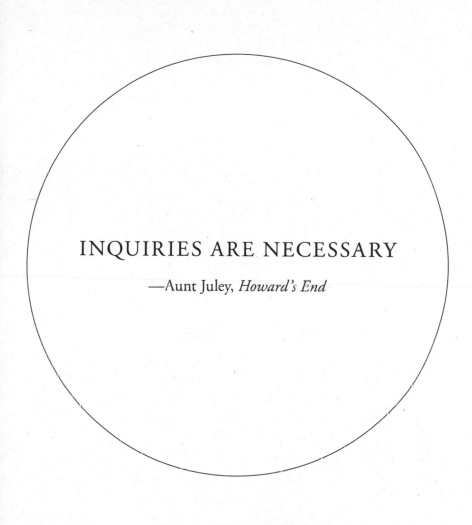

INQUIRIES ARE NECESSARY

—Aunt Juley, *Howard's End*

THAT'S THE NEXT PLACE TO WATCH

—L. B. Jefferies, *Rear Window*

KICK OFF YOUR SPURS

—Leslie Lynnton Benedict, *Giant*

CONSIDER THINGS
FROM [ANOTHER'S] POINT OF VIEW

—Atticus Finch, *To Kill a Mockingbird*

YOU'VE GOT IT

—Jett Rink, *Giant*

IT'S NOTHING LIKE YOU'VE EVER
GONE AFTER BEFORE

—Marcus Brody, *Raiders of the Lost Ark*

STAY OUT OF TROUBLE

—Robocop, *Robocop*

THAT'S JUST THE KIND YOU'VE GOT TO KEEP

—Chris Adams, *The Magnificent Seven*

[YOU] COULD DO DEEZ T'INGS

—Tony Manero, *Saturday Night Fever*

IF YOU GOTTA GO, GO WITH A SMILE

—The Joker, *Batman*

KEEP YOUR SWORDS BRIGHT
AND YOUR INTENTIONS TRUE

—Sheik Ilderim & Judah, *Ben-Hur*

SWITCH TO ANOTHER STATION

—Max Schumacher, *Network*

[DON'T] LET A BAD FIN STOP YOU

—Gill, *Finding Nemo*

DO SOMETHIN' BIGGER

—Lena, *A Raisin in the Sun*

SEPARATE THE FACTS FROM THE FANCY

—Judge, *12 Angry Men*

LAY OFF THE STUFF FOR AWHILE

—Nat, *The Lost Weekend*

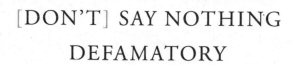

[DON'T] SAY NOTHING DEFAMATORY

—Mildred Hayes, *Three Billboards Outside Ebbing, Missouri*

ENJOY IT

—Joel, *Eternal Sunshine of the Spotless Mind*

IT HAS TO COME NATURALLY

—Victoria, *Victor/Victoria*

GET CLOSER

—Dr. Hannibal Lecter, *The Silence of the Lambs*

LOOK IN FRONT OF YOU

—Jack Griffin, *The Invisible Man*

YOU GOTTA GO WHERE THINGS HAPPEN

—Dave Hooch, *A League of Their Own*

KEEP IT BIG

—Jordan "Bick" Benedict Jr., *Giant*

MAKE YOUR MOVE

—Joel Goodson, *Risky Business*

TAKE NOTHING BUT THE BEST

—Tramp, *Lady and the Tramp*

[YOU] WON'T WANT CONVENTIONAL PROGRAMMING

—Diana Christensen, *Network*

PROTECT YOURSELF

—Serpico, *Serpico*

YES . . . YES, YES . . . YES, YES,
YEEESSS . . .
OOOHHHHH . . . YES, YES, YES!

—Sally, *When Harry Met Sally*

DON'T WORRY 'BOUT NUTIN'

—Tony Manero, *Saturday Night Fever*

DO SOMETHING TO HELP

—Helen Cooper, *Night of the Living Dead*

HEIGH-HO, HEIGH-HO, IT'S OFF TO WORK [YOU] GO

—Seven Dwarfs, *Snow White and the Seven Dwarfs*

[DON'T] IGNORE THE STRANGE
AND UNUSUAL

—Lydia Deetz, *Beetlejuice*

WELL THERE'S SOMETHING YOU DON'T SEE EVERY DAY

—Dr. Peter Venkman, *Ghostbusters*

WOULD IT BE INCONVENIENT?

—Macaulay (Mike) Connor, *The Philadelphia Story*

NO[THING]'S PERFECT

—Osgood E. Fielding III, *Some Like It Hot*

CHILL

—Love Daddy, *Do the Right Thing*

YOU'RE GOING TO GET IT

—Sebastian, *La La Land*

NO

—Jim Stark, *Rebel Without a Cause*

[IT'S] ALMOST PERFECT

—Barton Keyes, *Double Indemnity*

LUCKY FOR [YOU]

—Lestat de Lioncourt, *Interview with the Vampire*

DON'T TOUCH IT

—Q, *Goldfinger*

SURPRISE YOURSELF

—Lester Burnham, *American Beauty*

IT [COULD] MEAN EVERYTHING

—Anne, *Valley of the Dolls*

[IT] IS INTENDED
TO WHET YOUR APPETITE

—James Bond, *The Spy Who Loved Me*

CREATE A PLAUSIBLE DIVERSION

—Toddy, *Victor/Victoria*

DON'T GET DISCOURAGED

—Gay, *The Misfits*

[YOU] MIGHT LIKE A LITTLE
COMPANY

—Truman Burbank, *The Truman Show*

[DON'T] INVITE JUST ANYBODY

—Jena, *Pretty in Pink*

REARRANGE YOUR ALLIANCES

—George, *Who's Afraid of Virginia Woolf?*

GET PREPARED FOR IT

—Adam Bonner, *Adam's Rib*

YOU CAN NEVER LOSE
WHAT IT [WILL] GIVE YOU

—Mrs. Carrie Watts, *The Trip to Bountiful*

SOMEDAY IT [COULD] BE YOURS

—Inspector Clouseau, *The Pink Panther*

JUST KEEP SWIMMING,
JUST KEEP SWIMMING,
JUST KEEP SWIMMING

—Dory, *Finding Nemo*

SEE WHAT'S ON THE OTHER SIDE

—Robert Conway, *Lost Horizon*

MAKE THE BEST OF IT!

—Eric "Otter" Stratton, *Animal House*

I'M NOT SAYING
YOU WON'T GET YOUR HAIR
MUSSED

—General "Buck" Turgidson, *Dr. Strangelove or: How I Learned*

to Stop Worrying and Love the Bomb

I'M SORRY,
I DON'T HAVE ENOUGH
INFORMATION

—HAL 9000, *2001: A Space Odyssey*

EVERYTHING'S GONNA BE ALL RIGHT

—Sharon Waters, *My Own Private Idaho*

THIS IS GONNA STRIKE A SPECIAL
NERVE

—Wolfman Jack, *American Graffiti*

HOUSTON,
[YOU MAY] HAVE A PROBLEM

—Jim Lovell, *Apollo 13*

IT'S ONLY A MATTER OF TIME

—Prison Guard, *Papillon*

THE WHOLE HILL [WILL] SMELL
LIKE VICTORY

—Lieutenant Colonel Kilgore, *Apocalypse Now*

THIS IS [YOUR] MOMENT

—Aurora Greenway, *Terms of Endearment*

SIT THERE QUIETLY AND
COOPERATE

—Mrs. Iselin, *The Manchurian Candidate*

KEEP ALL YOUR HOMINY GRITS GOIN'
IN THE RIGHT DIRECTION

—Beauregard Burnside, *Auntie Mame*

GET ANOTHER SOURCE

—Howard Simons, *All the President's Men*

ALL GOOD THINGS TO THOSE
WHO WAIT

—Dr. Hannibal Lecter, *The Silence of the Lambs*

S'WONDERFUL, S'MARVELOUS

—Jerry Mulligan, *An American in Paris*

NOTHING'LL DO IT BUT YOUR
OWN SWEAT AND MUSCLE

—Joe Starrett, *Shane*

THINGS [COULD] CHANGE

—Carrie, *Carrie*

YOU MUST BE, OH SO SMART OR
OH SO PLEASANT
. . . . I RECOMMEND PLEASANT

—Elwood P. Dowd, *Harvey*

THERE'S NOTHING TO IT

—Linda Barrett, *Fast Times at Ridgemont High*

IT'S HEAVY

—Alisdair Stewart, *The Piano*

WHAT IS IT YOU'RE LOOKING FOR?

—Lisa Carol Fremont, *Rear Window*

[YOU] HAVE TO GO

—Gilbert Grape, *What's Eating Gilbert Grape*

[YOU'VE] GOT THE SAME CHANCE
AS ANYONE ELSE

—Charlie, *Willy Wonka and the Chocolate Factory*

YOU'VE BEEN GIVEN A GREAT GIFT

—Clarence, *It's a Wonderful Life*

SEE [THAT] EVERYTHING EXISTS
TOGETHER
IN A DELICATE BALANCE

—Mufasa, *The Lion King*

DON'T GIVE A HANG

—Dallas, *The Outsiders*

YOU KNOW WHAT YOU GOTTA DO, COWBOY

—Joe Buck, *Midnight Cowboy*

THE ANSWER'S OUT THERE
SOMEWHERE

—Lieutenant John Harper, *Plan 9 from Outer Space*

[DON'T] BE SENTIMENTAL

—John "Scottie" Ferguson, *Vertigo*

FLAUNT IT, BABY, FLAUNT IT!

—Max Bialystock, *The Producers*

[IT]'S LIKE MANURE, IT'S NOT
WORTH A THING
UNLESS [YOU] SPREAD [IT] AROUND

—Dolly Levi, *Hello, Dolly!*

[THAT'S] THE STUFF THAT
DREAMS ARE MADE OF

—Sam Spade, *The Maltese Falcon*

IF YOU'RE NOT LISTENING
CAREFULLY,
YOU [COULD] MISS THINGS

—Alan Turing, *The Imitation Game*

[YOU'LL] HAVE THINGS TO DO

—Bilbo Baggins, *Lord of the Rings: The Fellowship of the Ring*

YOU'LL FEEL BETTER IF YOU CAN
SEE [IT]

—Jack Griffin, *The Invisible Man*

[WHAT] YOU [ARE] LOOKING FOR
IS CLOSE

—Walter Neff, *Double Indemnity*

THINGS WILL WORK OUT

—Bud Stamper, *Splendor in the Grass*

GO AHEAD AND LAUGH

—Fanny Brice, *Funny Girl*

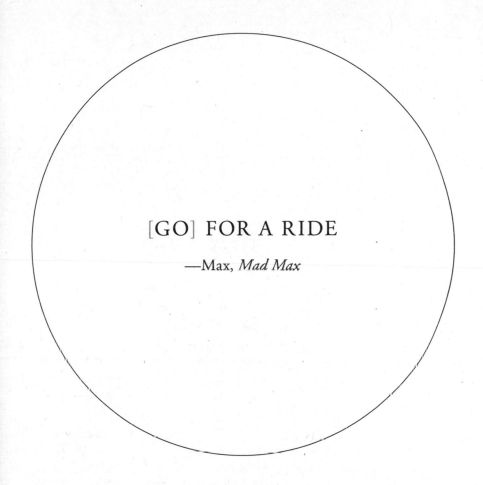

[GO] FOR A RIDE

—Max, *Mad Max*

YOU CAN MAKE IT

—Reverend Frank Scott, *The Poseidon Adventure*

[YOU] DESERVE RECOGNITION

—Mark Zuckerberg, *The Social Network*

[IT'S TIME TO] HAVE AN OLD
FRIEND
[OVER] FOR DINNER

—Dr. Hannibal Lecter, *The Silence of the Lambs*

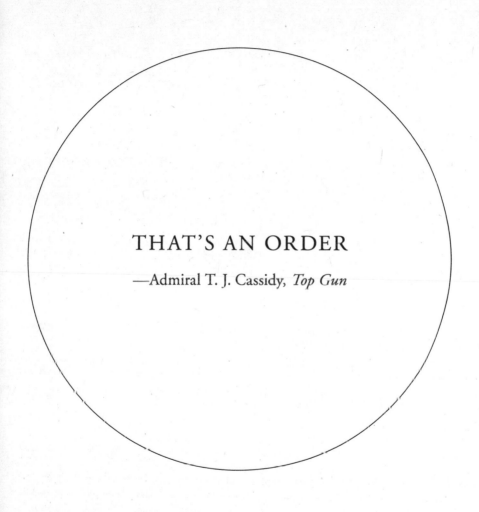

THAT'S AN ORDER

—Admiral T. J. Cassidy, *Top Gun*

IT'S GENUINE

—Christof, *The Truman Show*

SIMPLY REMEMBER [YOUR]

FAVORITE THINGS

—Maria, *The Sound of Music*

ANYTHING WORTH DOING

IS WORTH DOING RIGHT

—Jimmy Dugan, *A League of Their Own*

WE OUGHTA FILE THAT UNDER
"EDUCATIONAL,"
OUGHTN'T WE?

—Ellis "Red" Redding, *The Shawshank Redemption*

BE ON YOUR GUARD

—Frau Bäumer, *All Quiet on the Western Front*

GO ONE MOMENT MORE

—Karen, *Out of Africa*

CALL IT "[THE] PRIZE"

—Mr. Thomas Newton, *The Man Who Fell to Earth*

YEAH, WHY NOT?

—James Bond, *Goldfinger*

IT WILL PROTECT YOU

—Renfield's Mother, *Dracula*

IT'S ENOUGH

—Hobson, *Arthur*

BRAVO, BRAVO

—Alan Swann, *My Favorite Year*

[YOU] CAN FIX THAT

—Hubbell, *The Way We Were*

THINGS COULD BE BETTER

—Jack Torrance, *The Shining*

DON'T LET ANYONE TALK YOU OUT OF IT

—Julia, *Julia*

READY?

READY.

—Christine "Lady Bird" McPherson, *Lady Bird*

ANYTHING ABOUT IT SEEM
UNUSUAL TO YOU?

—Agent K, *Men in Black*

[YOU'VE GOT] ALL THE TIME IN THE WORLD

—Ellis "Red" Redding, *The Shawshank Redemption*

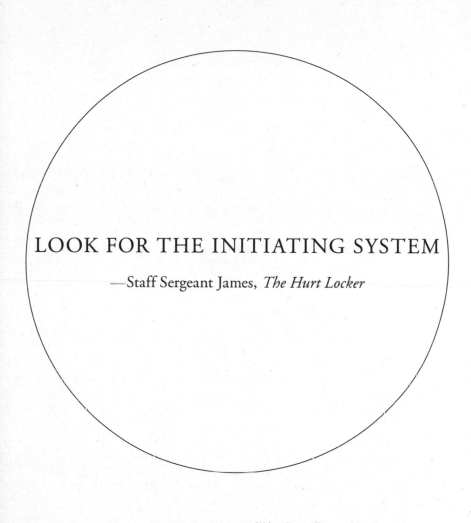

LOOK FOR THE INITIATING SYSTEM

—Staff Sergeant James, *The Hurt Locker*

[YOU ARE] JUST INCHES FROM A
CLEAN GETAWAY

—Garrett Breedlove, *Terms of Endearment*

THIS MEANS SOMETHING

—Roy Neary, *Close Encounters of the Third Kind*

YOU JUST GOTTA SEE YOURSELF
MAKIN' IT

—Paula, *An Officer and a Gentleman*

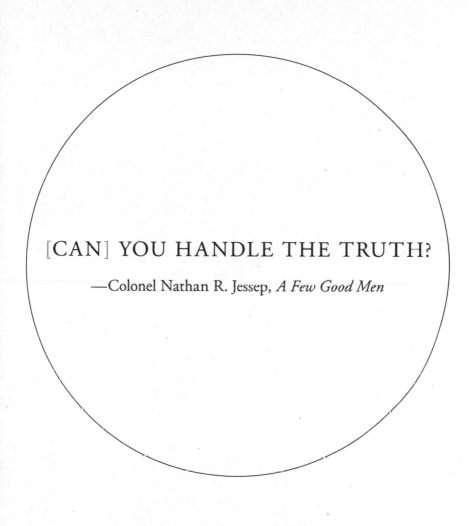

[CAN] YOU HANDLE THE TRUTH?

—Colonel Nathan R. Jessep, *A Few Good Men*

FOCUS, DUDE

—Crush, *Finding Nemo*

IT [COULD] BE A DETOUR

—Imperator Furiosa, *Mad Max: Fury Road*

TAKE A WALK

—Harlan Pepper, *Best in Show*

KEEP IT SAFE

—Gandalf, *Lord of the Rings: The Fellowship of the Ring*

[LOOK] FOR A SIGN TO CONTINUE
THE JOURNEY

—Pi, *Life of Pi*

BE REASONABLE

—Mark Thackeray, *To Sir, with Love*

CONSIDER IT A PUBLIC SERVICE

—D.A. Harvey Dent, *The Dark Knight*

HAVE YOU CHECKED YOUR FACTS?

—Bill Paley, *Good Night, and Good Luck*

IT'S A MYSTERY

—Philip Henslowe, *Shakespeare in Love*

THINK [ABOUT IT] DIFFERENTLY

Alan Turing, *The Imitation Game*

MAKE AN EXCEPTION OF YOURSELF

Master Ford, *12 Years a Slave*

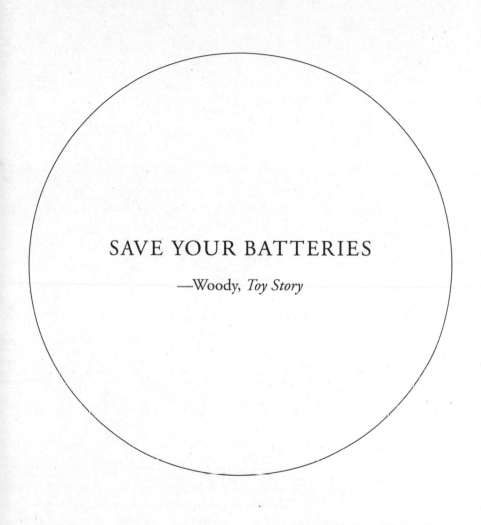

SAVE YOUR BATTERIES

—Woody, *Toy Story*

DO YOUR BEST

—Elastigirl, *The Incredibles*

HOW'S IT GOING TO LOOK?

—Tyler Winklevoss, *The Social Network*

THIS IS THE BEST BAD IDEA

—Jack O'Donnell, *Argo*

CONTROL YOUR POWERS

—Professor Xavier, *X-Men*

TALK ABOUT [THE] STANDARDS

—Dr. Theodore W. Milbank III, *Best in Show*

IT'S AN ADVENTURE!

—Carl and Ellie Fredricksen, *Up*

YOU [GOTTA] MAKE A MOVE

—Harry Osborn, *Spider-Man*

YOU'LL KNOW YOUR STRENGTHS
[AFTER THEY'VE] BEEN TESTED

—Pi, *Life of Pi*

YOU MUST KNOW THIS ONE

—Antonio Salieri, *Amadeus*

HOP ALONG

—Nick Wilde the Fox, *Zootopia*

[PUT] IT IN GEAR!

—Richard Hoover, *Little Miss Sunshine*

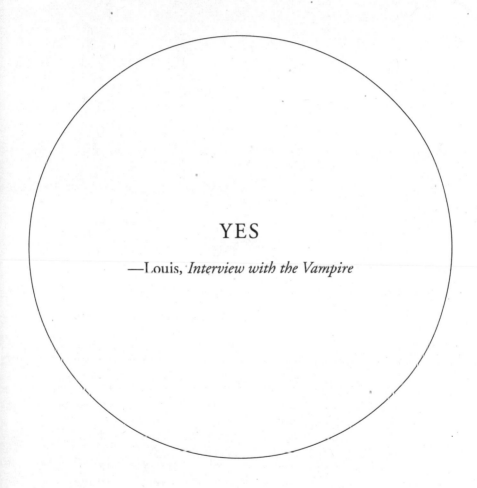

YES

—Louis, *Interview with the Vampire*

MAKE A DEAL

—Rayon, *Dallas Buyers Club*

[THIS COULD BE] THE START
OF SOMETHING WONDERFUL
AND NEW

—Sebastian, *La La Land*

[DON'T] FOCUS ON WHAT'S GOING WRONG

—Joy, *Inside Out*

[FIND A] FRIEND WHO LIKES TO PLAY!

—Bing Bong (Imagination), *Inside Out*

HAVE A GOOD TIME

—Mr. Robinson, *The Graduate*

THE RULES [MAY NOT] MAKE

ANY SENSE TO YOU

—Benjamin Braddock, *The Graduate*

[YOU'RE] NOT LAZY,
[MAYBE] YOU JUST DON'T CARE

—Peter Gibbons, *Office Space*

WATCH THAT FIRST STEP,
IT'S A DOOZY

—Ned, *Groundhog Day*

[YOU] GOT STUFF [YOU] HAVE
TO WORK OUT

—Andrew Largeman, *Garden State*

GET BUSY LIVING

—Ellis "Red" Redding, *The Shawshank Redemption*

TAKE PLEASURE IN THE DETAILS

—Troy Dyer, *Reality Bites*

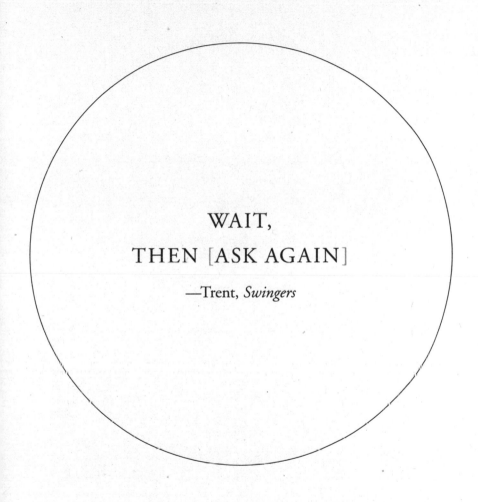

WAIT,

THEN [ASK AGAIN]

—Trent, *Swingers*

CHANGE THE WAY YOU LOOK

AT THINGS

—Christopher McCandless, *Into the Wild*

JUST LIVE BY THE ABCS: ADVENTUROUS, BRAVE, CURIOUS

—Walter Mitty, *The Secret Life of Walter Mitty*

IT'S SUPPOSED TO BE HARD, THE HARD IS WHAT MAKES IT GREAT

—Jimmy Dugan, *A League of Their Own*

YOUR FOCUS DETERMINES YOUR
REALITY

—Qui-Gon Jinn, *Star Wars: The Phantom Menace*

THIS IS A GREAT SCOUTING OPPORTUNITY

—Scout Master Ward, *Moonrise Kingdom*

BE THE VERY BEST VERSION OF
YOURSELF THAT YOU CAN BE

—Marion McPherson, *Lady Bird*

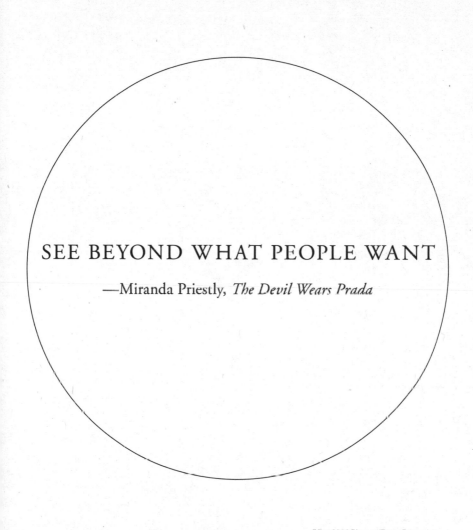

SEE BEYOND WHAT PEOPLE WANT

—Miranda Priestly, *The Devil Wears Prada*

CONFIRM AN APPOINTMENT

—Miranda Priestly, *The Devil Wears Prada*

KEEP THIS MEMORY

—Joel, *Eternal Sunshine of the Spotless Mind*

WHAT CAN YOU BRING TO IT
THAT NOBODY ELSE CAN?

—Mr. Turlington, *Boyhood*

[DON'T] BE TOO BUSY "TRYING"

—Charlie, *The Perks of Being a Wallflower*

COLLECT [MORE] INFORMATION

—Agent Williams, *Bridge of Spies*

EVERYTHING [WILL] COME FULL CIRCLE

—Carol Aird, *Carol*

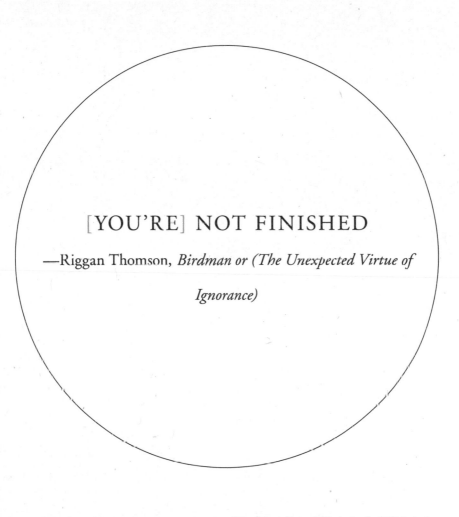

[YOU'RE] NOT FINISHED

—Riggan Thomson, *Birdman or (The Unexpected Virtue of*

Ignorance)

LONG PAUSES [CAN BE] GOOD

—Lionel Logue, *The King's Speech*

THERE'S GRIT IN IT

—Margaret Schlegel, *Howard's End*

IT [WILL] REMIND [YOU] OF ALL
THAT [IS] GOOD

—Terence Mann, *Field of Dreams*

ONE SHOULD [STAND UP]
FOR WHAT ONE BELIEVES

—Mark Thackeray, *To Sir, with Love*

THAT'S A MIGHTY BIG COMFORT

—O'Reilly, *The Magnificent Seven*

[MAKE] YOUR PLAYING PLAIN
AND TRUE

—Aunt Morag, *The Piano*

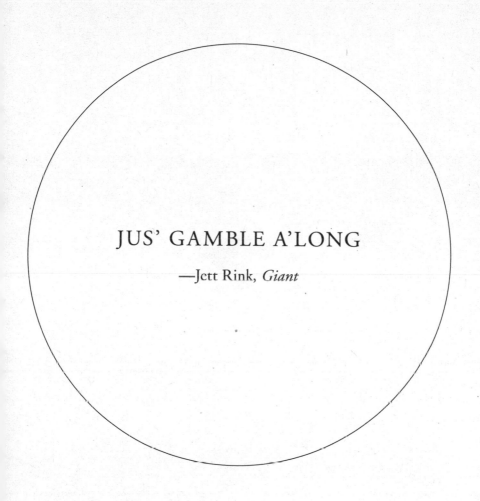

JUS' GAMBLE A'LONG

—Jett Rink, *Giant*

I THINK THAT'S POSSIBLE

—Juror 6, *12 Angry Men*

DON'T PLAY IT [TOO] SAFE

—Ronny Cammereri, *Moonstruck*

ACKNOWLEDGMENTS

Thank you to my agent Victoria Sanders and her Associates at Victoria Sanders Literary Agency: Bernadette, Jessica, and Diane. You took a chance on my project twenty years ago and it has been a pleasure ever since. I offer my deepest thanks and appreciation to you.

Hachette Books—Thank you to Amanda, Mollie, Becky, and Mauro for stretching into a new edition. I have loved the opportunity to dig around in some of my favorite places to find more answers: libraries and bookstores! I am sincerely grateful for your willingness to include me on the team to repackage a project that is so dear to me. Cheers to celebrating twenty years of having all the answers!

Thank you to the Seattle Public Library; every Seattle branch is my new favorite over and over again. My library card remains one of my most prized possessions.

And finally thank you to the creators of the text that is quoted. Your words in completion are an inspiration to me and I am grateful for the opportunity to use instances to create my books.